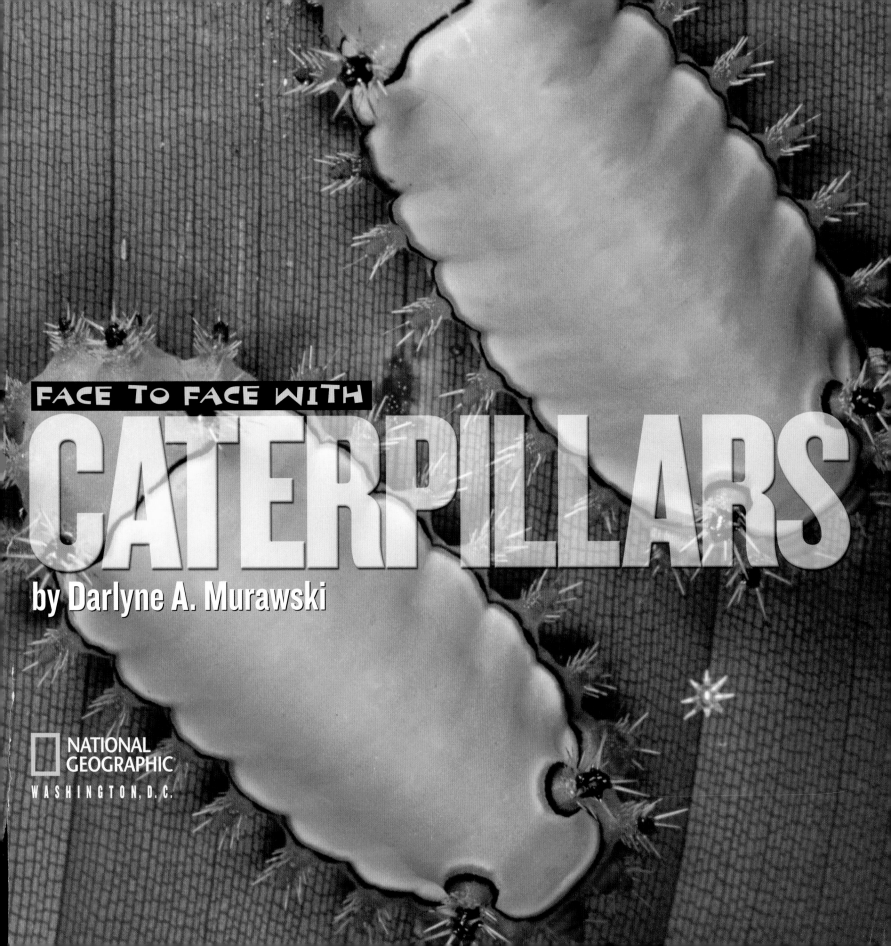

FACE TO FACE WITH
CATERPILLARS

by Darlyne A. Murawski

NATIONAL
GEOGRAPHIC
WASHINGTON, D.C.

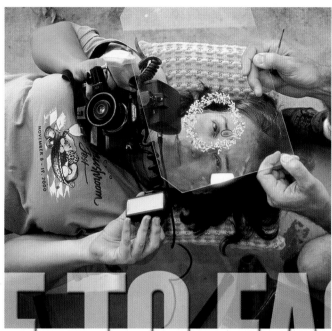

Here I am on my back photographing the caterpillar on the facing page.

FACE TO FACE

An Australian butterfly caterpillar eating an ant larva. Its diet consists entirely of young green tree ants. It lives inside the ant nests.

I was prying open a green tree ant nest with a brave biologist-assistant in Queensland, Australia. The summer heat was unbearable and the ants were biting like crazy, but we persisted. We eventually found our prize—a strange, rarely-seen caterpillar with a leathery body. It eats, of all things, young ants and lives exclusively in their nests.

The caterpillar's thick body seemed to glide like a vacuum cleaner over its prey. We transferred the

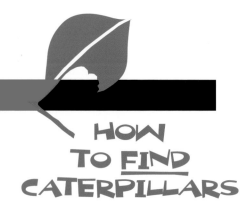

HOW TO FIND CATERPILLARS

- Look under leaves with holes or parts missing.
- Look inside leaves that are rolled and stitched shut with silk.
- Pick through the leaf litter on the ground.
- Search a vegetable garden, especially on cabbage, broccoli, and tomatoes.
- Use a field guide and get to know host plants. (For example, monarch caterpillars feed on milkweed.)
- Search tree trunks.

caterpillar and some ants to a glass plate so I could photograph them from below. I wanted to show how the caterpillar eats.

Later after many meals, the caterpillar got large and plump. It finally transformed into a beautiful butterfly. Then it had to quickly escape the ant nest before the ants could attack and kill it.

This was one of many surprising caterpillars that I encountered while on assignment for NATIONAL GEOGRAPHIC magazine. Each species has its own form, diet, defenses, habitat, and geographic range. To date, there are about 17,000 species of butterflies and 145,000 species of moths. And these are just the ones that have been described worldwide and given a scientific name. Many still await discovery.

Searching for caterpillars is like a treasure hunt. The harder they are to find, the more exciting the moment of discovery. You'll discover that some caterpillars live in large groups and make tents they all share. A few eat wax, pollen, or insects. Some spit acid or startle predators with a phony face. Others are so well camouflaged you can look right at them and not see them at all. Caterpillars are worth their weight in gold for all that they can teach us.

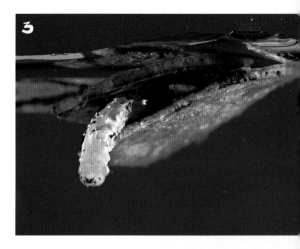

⬆ *A tiny sample of the caterpillars found worldwide shows how different caterpillars can look.*
1 *a tussock moth caterpillar from near San Jose, California,* **2** *a relative of* the monarch butterfly, a Euploea *caterpillar from Papua New Guinea,* **3** *the aquatic Sandwich man caterpillar from Florida,* **4** *a* Naprepa houla *moth caterpillar from Guanacaste,* Costa Rica, **5** *an unidentified pink moth caterpillar from central Panama, and* **6** *a Jelly Slug moth caterpillar from southeastern Arizona.*

MEET

THE CATERPILLAR

Imagine what it's like to grow up as an insect. You wouldn't have a skeleton inside you like people do, but you'd have one on the outside (an *exoskeleton,* which is also the skin). And instead of growing gradually, your body would go through distinct stages, each looking totally different from the previous stage. As a youngster, you'd be known as a caterpillar—a *larva,* or the second life stage of a butterfly or moth.

With camera poised to shoot, I watched a bumpy, dark caterpillar of the Priamus birdwing

butterfly. It laid down black silk from a needle-like gland below its head onto a green leaf.

The caterpillar was preparing to change into a *pupa*, one of its life stages. Once it finished its work, it attached the tail end of its body to the silk pad. Then it made a strong silk sling to help support the weight of its body. It slowly twisted, and its old skin peeled off, revealing the pupa (or *chrysalis*).

Inside the pupa, a most amazing transformation takes place. The old caterpillar body "melts down" and is reorganized as an adult butterfly. When the pupa is mature, the outer skin separates from the butterfly and splits open. The new adult slips out and hangs upside down. Blood flows through the veins of its limp, crumpled wings, forcing them to expand. After a few hours, the veins stiffen, and the butterfly can take wing for the first time. Moths undergo the same life changes, but the details may vary. Some moths also make a silk cocoon around their body just before they pupate.

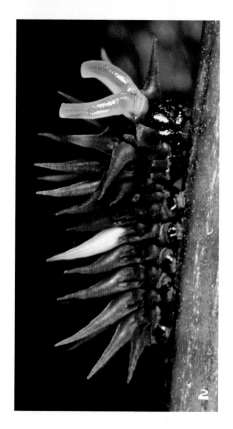

People constantly shed old skin cells and make new ones. But caterpillars have a toughened outer skin that gets too tight as they eat and grow. They have to shed their skin occasionally in a process

← *A tiny caterpillar of the Priamus birdwing butterfly from Papua New Guinea hatches from its egg (**1**) and eats its eggshell. If the caterpillar encounters a possible predator, it inflates a couple of orange fleshy horns over its head (**2**). These make unpleasant chemicals that scare off predators. It grows larger as it eats the leaves of its host plant (**3**). When the caterpillar is ready to turn into a pupa, it lays down a silk pad on a leaf and attaches itself to it. Then it makes a silk line to support the rest of its body. Inside the pupa (**4**), the caterpillar's organs are transformed into the adult butterfly's organs. Following this change, or metamorphosis, the adult butterfly emerges (**5**).*

HOW TO RAISE A MONARCH

— Get or make a caterpillar cage that can be cleaned and has air holes.

— Stock it with a cutting of a milkweed plant with fresh leaves and a monarch caterpillar.

— Empty the droppings in the trash and add fresh leaves each day.

— When the caterpillar gets large, put sticks in the cage so it can find a place to become a pupa.

— After one week, watch the pupa often to see the adult come out.

— Give the adult a day for its wings to stiffen without disturbing it, then release it outside.

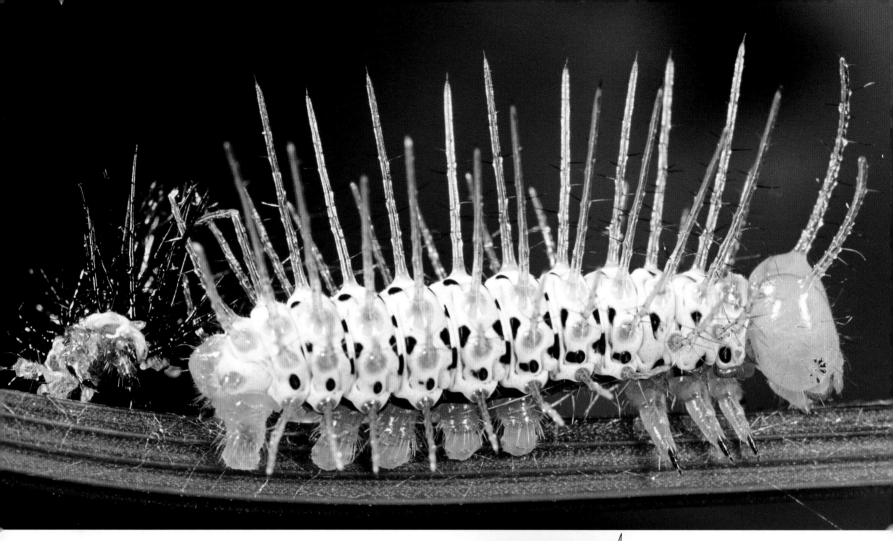

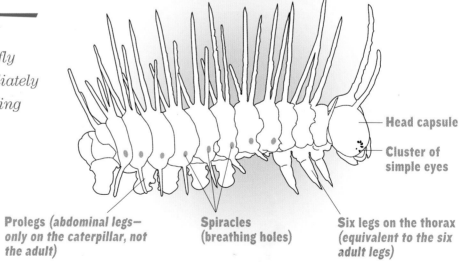

↑ *A caterpillar of a* Heliconius cydno *butterfly from Costa Rica immediately after molting, or shedding its skin.*

Head capsule

Cluster of simple eyes

Prolegs (abdominal legs—only on the caterpillar, not the adult)

Spiracles (breathing holes)

Six legs on the thorax (equivalent to the six adult legs)

called *molting*. Each stage between molts is called an *instar*. Caterpillars may go through four to seven instars before becoming a pupa. Later, as adults, they won't shed their skin anymore. And their bodies will begin to show signs of wear and tear as they age.

Caterpillars also see differently from us. They see only light and shadow through clusters of small eyes. When they become adults, they see what's around them very well through larger compound eyes.

Caterpillars eat by biting and chewing with jaws that open and shut like a pair of scissors. They will switch to a liquid diet as adults because all food must go up a soda straw–like *proboscis*.

Butterflies and moths in all life stages breathe through small holes on their sides called *spiracles*. Caterpillars have no lungs like ours, but air is forced in and out of their airways.

Caterpillars have many different outer forms. They can be smooth, hairy, spiny, bumpy, covered in gelatin, or with gills for breathing underwater.

Caterpillars may seem quite different from us, but we do have one thing in common. We both need to eat to live.

⬆ *A caterpillar eating a leaf. The hard mandibles (jaws) cut and chew the leaves.*

A newly hatched Heliconius *caterpillar* eats its own eggshell.

EATING MACHINES

A caterpillar needs the right kind of diet to survive. An egg-laying butterfly or moth will make an effort to find the right kind of host plant before laying her eggs. When an egg hatches, the new caterpillar usually eats its eggshell first. Then it eats the leaves and tender stems of its host plant.

Some caterpillars dine alone. Others feed in groups. They can strip an entire plant of its leaves.

Some caterpillars, like those of the gypsy moth, feed on many different kinds of host plants.

Limacodid caterpillars line up and feed on a vine leaf.

15

⬆ *A bizarre parasitic caterpillar looks like a white waxy blob. It feeds on an orange bug in northern India—weakening, but not killing, its host.*

Others have very fussy diets. They may only be able to eat one or just a few kinds of plants. There are caterpillars who can even eat poisonous host plants. They are not harmed by the plants' poisons. Instead the plants' poisons make the caterpillars taste bad to animals who try to eat them.

Not all caterpillars eat leaves. Some will eat flower parts, beeswax (a specialty of the "wax

worm" caterpillar), and even insects. I've seen caterpillars (like the one at far left) make host bugs both their homes and their dinner. Other caterpillars (like the one above) aren't so lucky, and become dinner themselves.

To eat but not be eaten is the name of the game. Being low on the food chain, caterpillars encounter lots of threats. Let's see how they deal with them.

A doomed hornworm moth caterpillar on a tomato plant is covered with wasp cocoons. These wasp larvae feed on the inside of the caterpillar, slowly killing it.

A spicebush swallowtail caterpillar from Cape Cod with false eyes.

SELF-DEFENSE

A monkey slug caterpillar from Costa Rica has false spidery legs that can break off when a predator attacks it.

Caterpillars are masters of self-defense. They need to be since the odds are against them. They are food for lots of other animals. Most caterpillars are eaten before reaching adulthood. But some will make it, because they have adapted clever ways to survive.

In the field, I've come face-to-face with some startling caterpillars. But when I looked closer, I realized their faces were phony. When threatened, they tuck their real heads under and flash a false face with big eyes to scare animals, especially birds—and me!

A passing bird might mistake a monkey slug caterpillar for a large, hairy spider. But once the bird attacks, it's in for a surprise. The caterpillar detaches its false legs to protect the main part of its body.

Many caterpillars rely on camouflage to avoid being seen. Some look like their background— whether it's a twig, a leaf, a flower, moss, or lichen. The opposite strategy is to stand out like a sore thumb. Caterpillars with bright colors are advertising their bad taste so that predators will avoid them.

I encountered a spiny, transparent caterpillar in Costa Rica. As I prepared my camera to shoot, I accidentally brushed its spines with the back of my hand and felt a stinging chemical. The intense pain that followed didn't let up for a good 20 minutes. That's a vivid reminder to keep away!

The puss moth caterpillar (*see picture page 9*) uses another form of chemical self-defense. It spits

➡ An inchworm crawls up a tree branch in Ohio. Its shape and coloration gives it the appearance of a stick.

When the caterpillar rests, it stretches out and looks like a branch.

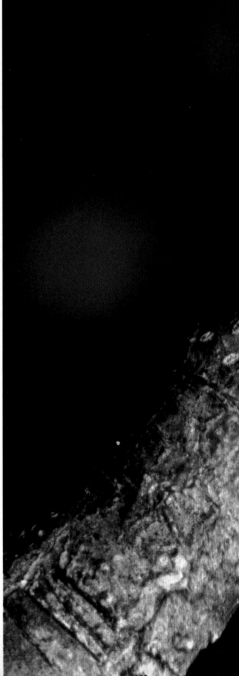

A skipper caterpillar from Costa Rica makes a temporary shelter by rolling a leaf and stitching it partly shut.

HOW TO SEE LIKE A CATERPILLAR

- Face a bright light such as a computer screen or light bulb.

- Close your eyes.

- Pass one hand back and forth in front of your eyes slowly.

- Notice that all you can see is light and shadow, but no shapes.

formic acid into the eyes of its enemies. The acid comes from a gland just below the caterpillar's head. What's more, it waves two rubbery pink tentacles that release an odor to keep predators away.

Caterpillars might hide during the day in the leaf litter on the ground. Or they might cling to the underside of leaves where passing birds won't see them. They may even use silk in their defense. When threatened, small caterpillars often bungee-jump from a silk thread attached to a leaf or branch. When the caterpillar is finished reeling out silk, it waits a while in midair then climbs back up "hand over hand," gathering up the thread to re-use it.

Some caterpillars called "leaf rollers" use their silk to curl a leaf and stitch it shut so they can hide inside. Tent caterpillars work together to build a communal tent. If the tent isn't enough for protection, they wriggle as a group—thrashing

1 A Euclea *moth caterpillar from Costa Rica (seen from below) has hollow needles packed with a stinging fluid.* **2** *A young eastern tent caterpillar "bungee-jumped" off a* cherry leaf to escape a threat. Here it climbs back up its line, gathering up silk on the way. **3** Eastern tent caterpillars and the silk tent they built together.

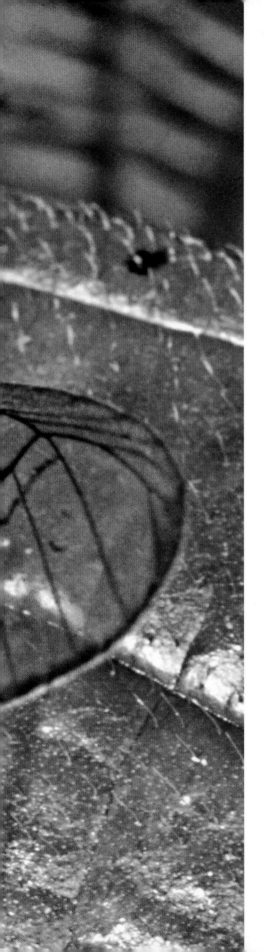

← *When we see a winged adult, we can appreciate that it is one of the few that beat the odds.*

from side to side. A loud noise can set them off. If a predator grabs hold of a tent caterpillar, watch out. The caterpillar will vomit a toxic chemical.

Bag worm caterpillars also make an elaborate silk shelter—one they wear to hide their body. They decorate the bag with twigs, leaves, or lichens to blend in with their environment.

Some caterpillars live with ants. They either have a thick body that ants can't attack or they fool ants into caring for them. Some feed the ants nectar.

Caterpillars are tiny insects living in a dangerous world. But they respond and adapt to meet the many challenges. Each caterpillar feeds and fends off predators in order to survive and make the big change, its metamorphosis into a butterfly or moth. When I see a winged adult, I know it survived the odds. Growing up can be hard—even for caterpillars! To see them finally take flight is a beautiful thing.

HOW YOU CAN HELP

⬆ *Alcon blue butterfly*

WE'VE SEEN HOW THE caterpillar is just one stage in the life of a butterfly or moth. During its lifetime its needs, such as food and proper habitat (the place where a butterfly or moth is found in nature), must be met. Each species needs different things to survive.

Take the rare Alcon blue butterfly, for example. It starts its life on a marsh gentian flower growing in Europe. When a tiny caterpillar hatches from its egg, it eats the inside of the flower. But after it grows a bit and molts, it drops off the plant. Then a certain type of ant carries it into its nest and feeds it just like it feeds its own larvae.

The Alcon blue caterpillar requires the right kind of habitat with the right plant and the right ant, or it won't survive. The adult butterfly has a different diet from the caterpillar. It needs the right flowers for its nectar.

Changes in habitat and loss of habitat are the main problems for the Alcon blue, as they are for many butterflies and moths. Butterfly and moth habitats need to be created and preserved.

How can you help out?

━ Plant a garden. A few plants with flowers that attract and feed butterflies and moths are milkweed, butterfly weed, verbenas, and more.

━ Using a field guide, find out which butterflies and moths live in your area. Try growing the caterpillars' host plants in your yard or school grounds. Help to protect the host plants in your area.

━ Read up on butterflies and moths that might be rare or uncommon in your area. Learn about their special needs and habitats. Tell parents, teachers, and local conservation officials of your interest in protecting the future of those species. Then work with them to plan your course of action.

IT'S YOUR TURN

YOUR ASSIGNMENT is to write, photograph, or illustrate a book or article on caterpillars. The pictures and writing should be engaging. What would you like to learn about a caterpillar that lives in your area? What would you like to tell your readers about this caterpillar? Here's a checklist of caterpillar behaviors to help you. Watch quietly and patiently and see how many behaviors you can check off on this list.

CHECKLIST
- Eating
- Molting
- Caterpillar hatching from its egg
- Caterpillar turning into a pupa
- Adult coming out of its pupal skin
- Caterpillar crawling or wandering
- Caterpillar protecting itself from a predator
- Caterpillar making a silk line or silk structure
- A parasite laying eggs on or inside a caterpillar
- A parasite emerging from a caterpillar's body
- A caterpillar being attacked by predators

Now you're ready to write, photograph, or draw what you've seen. Good luck!

← *A butterfly garden (left) is a good place to look for caterpillars, moths, and butterflies such as the monarch butterfly (middle and top).*

FACTS AT A GLANCE

▲ *Cecropia moth and its caterpillar*

Common and scientific names

People use common names to refer to caterpillars, but these can differ around the world. Scientists try to use the same name to refer to a species, no matter where they are. This is called its scientific name. For example, scientists call the monarch butterfly, *Danaus plexippus.*

Diet

Most caterpillars eat leaves of one or more types of plant and are considered herbivores (plant eaters). Some caterpillars eat insects and are considered either predators (if they kill their prey) or parasites (if they weaken but don't kill their host).

▼ *Caterpillars live all over the world.*

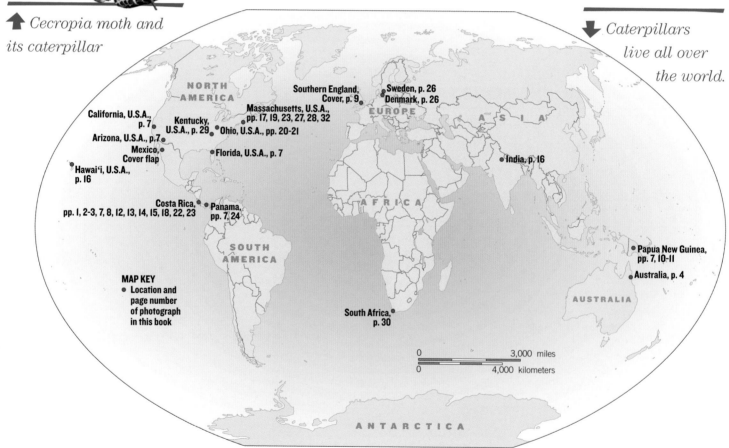

California, U.S.A., p. 7

Kentucky, U.S.A., p. 29

Arizona, U.S.A., p. 7

Mexico, Cover flap

Florida, U.S.A., p. 7

Hawai'i, U.S.A., p. 16

Costa Rica, pp. 1, 2-3, 7, 8, 12, 13, 14, 15, 18, 22, 23

Panama, pp. 7, 24

Southern England, Cover, p. 9

Massachusetts, U.S.A., pp. 17, 19, 23, 27, 28, 32

Ohio, U.S.A., pp. 20-21

Sweden, p. 26

Denmark, p. 26

India, p. 16

Papua New Guinea, pp. 7, 10-11

Australia, p. 4

South Africa, p. 30

NORTH AMERICA
SOUTH AMERICA
EUROPE
ASIA
AFRICA
AUSTRALIA
ANTARCTICA

MAP KEY
• Location and page number of photograph in this book

0   3,000 miles
0   4,000 kilometers

Habitat

Caterpillars live in many different kinds of habitats, depending on the species. They can live in rain forests, meadows, deserts, gardens, and even underwater.

Range

Caterpillars can be found living on every continent of the Earth, except Antarctica.

Life cycle

Caterpillars have four stages in their life cycle: egg, larva (caterpillar), pupa, and adult (butterfly or moth).

Number of species

The approximate number of species with scientific names is 17,000 for butterflies and 145,000 for moths.

Caterpillar silk

Caterpillars produce a strand of silk that is used for various purposes such as cocoon-making in some moths, stitching leaves together, making various kinds of shelters or body covers, dropping out of the sight of a potential predator, and ballooning (making a long line to disperse by wind to another location). The silk dries upon contact with the air.

Breathing

Caterpillars, like most insects, breathe through air holes in their bodies called spiracles. Oxygen and carbon dioxide are exchanged inside a system of tubes that run through the caterpillar's body.

Kinds of defenses

Caterpillars have various defenses against predators and parasites. Hiding and making shelters are two main defenses. Other defenses include false faces, spines, leathery bodies, detachable false legs, and many kinds of visual mimicry, or camouflage. Defenses that use chemicals include squirting acid and incorporating bad-tasting chemicals from a host plant into the caterpillar's body to keep predators from eating it.

⬆ *Luna Moth*

Differences between butterflies and moths

The main differences are seen in the adults. The easiest part to identify is the antennae, which are knobbed at the tips in butterflies and are either feathery or straight in moths. Butterflies fly during the day. Most moths fly at night. At rest, butterflies close their wings over their backs. Moths hold their wings open or in other positions. All caterpillars will change into either a butterfly or a moth, so long as they survive to metamorphosis.

GLOSSARY

Camouflage: concealment; using shape or coloration to blend in with one's surroundings

Caterpillar: the larval stage of a butterfly or moth

Chrysalis: another word for a butterfly pupa

Exoskeleton: an outside covering or support for the body

Host plant: a plant that caterpillars eat. A butterfly or moth will lay its eggs on a host plant.

Instar: the stage when a caterpillar is between molts

Larva: an immature stage of an insect with a complete metamorphosis. In butterflies and moths, the larva is also called a caterpillar.

Life cycle: the different stages in an organism's life. The first stage is when life begins and the final stage happens when the organism can reproduce and have young.

Metamorphosis: a change in shape and habits, such as when a caterpillar becomes a moth or butterfly

Molting: the action of shedding

Proboscis: flexible tube of a moth or butterfly, used for sucking

Prolegs: small, paired, leg-like stumps along a caterpillar's body that help it move

Pupa: the resting stage between the caterpillar and the adult

Species: a group of living things that look like one another and are able to reproduce with each other

Spiracles: small holes along a caterpillar's body through which it breathes

Thorax: the middle part of the body of an insect, between the head and abdomen

FIND OUT MORE

Articles & Books

"Moths Come to Light." NATIONAL GEOGRAPHIC magazine, Mar. 1997, pp. 40–57.

⬆ *A South African caterpillar being fed by an ant.*

"Parasites: Looking for a Free Lunch." NATIONAL GEOGRAPHIC magazine, Oct. 1997, pp. 74–91.

"Killer Caterpillars: Built to Eat Flesh." NATIONAL GEOGRAPHIC magazine, June 2003, pp. 100–111.

Peterson First Guide to Caterpillars of North America, by Amy Bartlett Wright. Houghton Mifflin, 1993, revised 1998. *It's important to have a good field guide.*

Web sites

http://insected.arizona.edu/bflyinfo.htm *Butterfly and moth information*

http://www.butterfliesandmoths.org/ *A chance to look up butterflies and moths from your area*

http://www.eenorthcarolina.org/garden/butterflyhowto.htm *Tips on raising your own caterpillars*

http://www.tooter4kids.com/LifeCycle/General_Information.htm *Butterfly anatomy*

http://www.thewildones.org/Animals/monarch.html *Monarch life cycle*

http://whatsthatbug.com/caterpillar_2.html *Help with caterpillar identification*

INDEX

Boldface indicates illustrations.

RESEARCH & PHOTOGRAPHIC NOTES

Caterpillars are fun to photograph because if you're reasonably careful, they won't hide from you, hurt you, or crawl away. The hard part is finding them, especially since many are well-camouflaged. I usually consult with local experts who know of locations to find my subjects and who may accompany me in the field. When I'm away from home, I often stay at field stations located at the site. That way I'm near the habitats where I want to search for caterpillars.

In the field I usually don't use much (if any) insect repellent. I carry lots of camera equipment, mostly macro (close-up) lenses and several flash units, plus diffusers, reflectors and other gadgets to get the photos I want. I have to search slowly for caterpillars, looking all over, especially on plants. Once I find my subject, it might still take a long time to get the photos. The adult butterflies and moths are more difficult to shoot. I have to sneak up on them very slowly. Most of the caterpillars and adult butterflies and moths I shot for this book were in the wild. But the South African Thestor caterpillar and its tending ants on p. 30 came from a biologist who was working on that species, and the monarch caterpillar came from a local butterfly exhibit.

Each type of butterfly or moth has a scientific name. For young children, the names can be long or difficult to read. But I know a few children might enjoy looking up more information on certain species—perhaps for school projects, or just for the fun of it. So here's a partial list of scientific names by page number.

Cover and p. 9, *Cerura vinula;* Front flap, *Xylophanes falco;* Title page, *Acharia ophelians;* p. 4, *Liphyra brassolis;* p. 7 (3), *Synclita obliterata;* p. 7 (4), *Dalcerides ingenita;* pp. 10-11, *Troides priamus;* p. 16 left, *Epiricania melanoleuca;* p. 16 right, *Eupithecia staurophragma;* p. 17, *Manduca sexta;* p. 18, *Phobetron hipparchia;* p. 19, *Papilio troilus;* p. 23 and p. 32, *Malacosoma americanum;* p. 24, *Cithaerias menander;* p. 26, *Maculinea alcon;* p. 27, *Danaus plexippus;* p. 28, *Hyalophora cecropia;* p. 29, *Actias luna;* p 30, a species of the genus *Thestor.* —DM

FOR SARAH. —DM

Acknowledgments:
I'd like to thank the many people and organizations that have helped facilitate the research projects and photographic articles over the last 20 plus years that have led to the making of this book. Special thanks to Rod Eastwood, Naomi Pierce, David Lohman, Stephen Montgomery, Don Davis, Marc Epstein, Don Harvey, Lawrence Gilbert, Daniel Janzen and the INBIO project, Dale Habeck, Alan Heath, Charles Covell, Jr., David Nash, Thomas Als, and Per Stadl Nielsen for sharing their knowledge and expertise at various times. Thanks to David Lohman for providing the photo of me on page 5. I am grateful to the Costa Rican National Park Service, the Smithsonian Tropical Research Institute in Panama, the Asociación Nacional para la Conservación de la Naturaleza (in Panama), the Simbhaoli Sugar Plantation (in India), the Australian Insect Farm in Garradunga (Queensland), the Butterfly Place in Westford, MA, the Southwestern Research Station in Arizona, among others, for their part.—DM

Art p.12 by Stuart Armstrong; *Back cover photograph* by Becky Hale/National Geographic Society; *p. 5 photograph* by David Lohman

⬆ *Look for tent caterpillars making silk shelters in trees.*

Published by the
National Geographic Society

John M. Fahey, Jr., *President and Chief Executive Officer*

Gilbert M. Grosvenor, *Chairman of the Board*

Nina D. Hoffman, *Executive Vice President, President of Books*

Staff for This Book

Nancy Laties Feresten, *Vice President, Editor-in-Chief of Children's Books*

Bea Jackson, *Design and Illustrations Director, Children's Books*

Jennifer Emmett, *Project Editor*

David M. Seager, *Art Director*

Lori Epstein, *Illustrations Editor*

Michelle Harris, *Researcher*

Jean Cantu, *Illustrations Specialist*

Carl Mehler, *Director of Maps*

Rebecca Baines, *Editorial Assistant*

R. Gary Colbert, *Production Director*

Lewis R. Bassford, *Production Manager*

Vincent P. Ryan, *Manufacturing Manager*

Book design by David M. Seager
The body text of the book is set in ITC Century. The display text is set in Knockout and Party Noid.

Front cover: A false-face puss moth caterpillar. *Front flap:* A falcon sphinx moth caterpillar. *Back cover:* The author gets face to face with a milkweed tussock moth caterpillar. *Page one:* A sphinx moth caterpillar nibbles a leaf. *Title page:* Blue-nose caterpillars from Costa Rica.

Library of Congress
Cataloging-in-Publication Data

Murawski, Darlyne A.
 Face to face with caterpillars / by Darlyne A. Murawski.
   p. cm. -- (Face to face)
 Includes bibliographical references and index.
  ISBN-13: 978-1-4263-0052-3 (hardcover)
  ISBN-13: 978-1-4263-0053-0 (library binding)
 1. Caterpillars. I. Title.
 QL544.M87 2006
 595.78'139--dc22

2006020499

Printed in China